THE CLIMATE CRISIS IN THE NORTHWEST AND ALASKA

by Brienna Rossiter

WWW.FOCUSREADERS.COM

Copyright © 2024 by Focus Readers®, Lake Elmo, MN 55042. All rights reserved. No part of this book may be reproduced or utilized in any form or by any means without written permission from the publisher.

Focus Readers is distributed by North Star Editions:
sales@northstareditions.com | 888-417-0195

Produced for Focus Readers by Red Line Editorial.

Content Consultant: Julie C. Padowski, PhD, Research Associate Professor, School of the Environment, Washington State University

Photographs ©: Shutterstock Images, cover, 1, 8–9, 13, 14–15, 22–23, 26; John Froschauer/AP Images, 4–5; Nathan Howard/AP Images, 7; Red Line Editorial, 11; Kevin Jantzer/AP Images, 17; Shawn Harrison/Pacific Coastal and Marine Science Center/USGS, 19; JS Photo/Alamy, 21; Tech. Sgt. Daniel J. Martinez/147th Attack Wing Public Affairs/Texas Air National Guard/DVIDS, 24; iStockphoto, 29

Library of Congress Cataloging-in-Publication Data
Library of Congress Cataloging-in-Publication Data is available on the Library of Congress website.

ISBN
978-1-63739-632-2 (hardcover)
978-1-63739-689-6 (paperback)
978-1-63739-797-8 (ebook pdf)
978-1-63739-746-6 (hosted ebook)

Printed in the United States of America
Mankato, MN
082023

ABOUT THE AUTHOR
Brienna Rossiter is a writer and editor who lives in Minnesota.

TABLE OF CONTENTS

CHAPTER 1
Extreme Heat 5

CHAPTER 2
Typical Climate 9

CHAPTER 3
Rising Risks 15

THAT'S AMAZING!
Preserving First Foods 20

CHAPTER 4
Taking Action 23

Focus on the Northwest and Alaska • 30
Glossary • 31
To Learn More • 32
Index • 32

CHAPTER 1

EXTREME HEAT

In 2021, a heat wave hit the US Northwest. Temperatures in several states climbed to record highs. Seattle, Washington, reached 108 degrees Fahrenheit (42°C). Portland, Oregon, peaked at 116 degrees Fahrenheit (47°C). Some inland areas got even hotter.

In 2021, a heat wave brought record-high temperatures to Washington, Oregon, and Idaho. Some people stayed in cooling centers.

It was so hot that some power lines melted. Streets cracked. Many crops withered and died. Ocean water heated up, too. Hundreds of thousands of sea creatures died.

Many buildings didn't have air-conditioning. Hospitals filled with people who had heat-related illnesses.

ALREADY INCREASING

Heat waves used to be rare in the Northwest. But the 2021 wave broke records set in 2015. Another heat wave came in 2022. That wave didn't get as hot. But it lasted longer. Longer heat waves put more stress on people and animals. They also put more stress on **infrastructure**.

Some companies forced farmworkers in the Northwest to work through the heat wave. At least one farmworker died.

By the heat wave's end, more than 200 people in the Northwest had died.

The extreme heat happened because of **climate change**. Climate experts warned that events like this could become more common if people did not take action.

CHAPTER 2

TYPICAL CLIMATE

The Pacific Northwest is known for being rainy. Parts of this region do get many days of rain each year. But for the rest of the region, the amount of rain that falls tends to be low. Instead, areas east of the Cascade Range get most of their water in the form of snow. In fact, most of the Northwest's **precipitation** falls in

The Rocky Mountains cover much of Idaho. As a result, the state's climate varies a lot.

winter. That means that snow provides an important source of water.

East of the Cascades, summers can become very hot. But along the coast, temperatures are usually mild. Summers tend to be warm and dry. Winters are cool. Warm ocean waters keep temperatures from dropping as much.

CASCADE RAIN SHADOW

The Cascade Range creates a rain shadow. Air moving in from the ocean must rise to go over the mountains. As it rises, the air gets colder. This causes the air's moisture to fall as rain or snow. By the time the air sinks down the other side of the mountains, it's drier. So, that area tends to stay dry during most of the year.

Being close to the ocean has other impacts. The region is affected by El Niño and La Niña. These weather patterns tend

THE NORTHWEST AND ALASKA

to happen every few years. They happen when the Pacific Ocean's temperatures change. El Niño makes the Northwest hotter and drier than usual. La Niña can bring heavy rain and flooding.

Alaska's climate is also impacted by the ocean. Conditions throughout the large state vary. Coastal areas tend to be milder. But northern and inland areas can get very cold. In fact, much of the state is covered in permafrost. This layer of the ground is frozen solid all year. Northern areas are covered in snow for much of the year. They also have glaciers and sea ice.

The Northwest is known for its forests and farmland. Many people depend

Arctic areas in Alaska are home to many plants and animals. Few other areas on Earth have these habitats.

on these resources. That includes the region's **Indigenous** peoples. The Lummi people of Washington are one example. They have caught and cared for salmon for thousands of years. Tribes living near Colville National Forest in Washington are another. They use controlled burns to prevent wildfires.

CHAPTER 3

RISING RISKS

Climate change is already causing many serious problems in the Northwest. Since 1900, the region's average temperatures have risen. By 2020, most places had warmed by 2 degrees Fahrenheit (1.1°C). Alaska is warming even faster. If this shift continues, heat waves will likely become more common.

Warmer weather can help invasive insects spread. The mountain pine beetle has damaged forests in the Northwest.

So will droughts. Both events can kill crops and cause food shortages.

Hot, dry weather helps wildfires start and spread. In 2015, for example, the Northwest had record-high temperatures. Massive wildfires burned across Oregon and Washington. Smoke polluted the air in surrounding states, including Idaho.

Other problems are related to snow. As snow melts, water flows into lakes, streams, and rivers. But these bodies of water can run low if snow melts earlier or if less snow falls. Water may also get warmer. This can kill fish such as salmon.

Near Alaska, the ocean has grown warmer. **Ocean acidity** is also increasing.

In September 2020, wildfires in the Northwest destroyed five towns and burned huge areas of land.

As a result, sea creatures are dying. Warmer water can also lead to harmful algal blooms. These huge patches of algae can kill fish. Some also release **toxins**.

Meanwhile, ice and permafrost are melting. Permafrost lies under much of the ground in Alaska. When it melts, the ground becomes unstable. Roads and buildings can sink or collapse. Melting permafrost also releases carbon. The carbon enters the atmosphere as greenhouse gases. These gases trap heat in Earth's atmosphere. So, melting permafrost can lead to even more climate change.

 Melting ice and warmer water also cause ocean levels to rise. Coastal areas can face flooding or erosion. And when ice melts, animals lose their homes. As temperatures rise, some animals may move farther north. This shift can affect **ecosystems** in many ways.

Permafrost melts in northern Alaska.

All of these changes can be hard to notice day-to-day. They happen slowly. But the shifts are serious. Over time, they add up to a crisis. Plus, climate change can become even worse. Then, extreme weather events will be more common.

THAT'S AMAZING!

PRESERVING FIRST FOODS

Indigenous peoples have depended on certain foods for thousands of years. These foods are often known as First Foods. They are a core part of many Indigenous cultures. So are the rights to harvest them. These rights were often key parts of treaties. Indigenous nations signed these treaties with the US government. However, the government broke many of these agreements. Some nations now struggle to access their First Foods.

Activists are working to fix this problem. Valerie Segrest is a member of the Muckleshoot Indian Tribe in Washington. She focuses on helping communities access First Foods. In 2009, she launched a new project. It hosts events that

Salmon is one of the First Foods of the Muckleshoot Indian Tribe.

share traditional knowledge. Some events teach people to gather nettles and berries. Others show ways to catch and cook mussels and salmon.

In many Indigenous cultures, plants and animals are seen as teachers. They offer ways of living that are good for both people and the land.

CHAPTER 4

TAKING ACTION

Greenhouse gas emissions are the main cause of climate change. Reducing them is key. But it will not be enough. Some changes are already happening.

In fact, some places are becoming unsafe to live. For example, Newtok is a town on Alaska's coast. The Yup'ik people live there. In the 2000s, storms

In 2022, Washington State said it would ban sales of new gasoline cars by 2035. This move aimed to lower greenhouse gas emissions.

In 2019, the US National Guard helped build homes in a new town. People relocated there from Newtok, Alaska.

flooded Newtok several times. Many buildings were destroyed. Land eroded. Sewage entered the water supply, making water unsafe to drink. Residents started evacuating in 2019. If climate change continues, more people could lose their homes.

In other areas, people are adapting to the climate crisis. For example, algal blooms in Alaska put shellfish harvesters at risk. In response, the Sitka Tribe created a shellfish testing lab. This lab collects data. It also does weekly studies. Lab workers share this information with scientists. Together, they watch for problems. They also let harvesters know when shellfish aren't safe to keep.

Other groups bring people together. One helps tribes access research and funding. In this way, people can find better ways to protect the environment. In Idaho, public health workers teamed up with local tribes and universities. They

Wildfire smoke can harm people's health. It can make lung and heart conditions worse.

studied water shortages and wildfire smoke. They worked on limiting the harm from those problems.

Engineers also design and test new tools. These tools collect data. People can use those data to track change. They show which areas will be most harmed by climate change. The tools often use climate models. These models look at a region's temperature patterns. They look at precipitation patterns, too. The models show how the climate might respond to more greenhouse gases or other changes.

Models usually run on powerful computers. But these computers are costly. Groups of volunteers can help. They share their personal computers. Shared computers work together to run models. Scientists can help leaders use this information to plan for the future.

Cities and governments are taking action, too. The city of Boise, Idaho, built a water treatment plant. The plant controls how much phosphorus enters rivers. That way, the region's water stays cleaner. In Seattle and Portland, community groups are supporting people's health. They focus on low-income people and people of color.

DOWNSCALING

Many climate models show large parts of the globe. But leaders usually make plans for just one region. For this reason, they need specific details about the area. Focusing a model on one particular region is called downscaling. Downscaled models can predict many things. These might be heat waves or how many days will be stormy. They can also show how severe droughts or flooding might be. This information helps leaders know how to prepare.

Costly housing in Portland has increased homelessness. Unhoused people are vulnerable to extreme weather.

These groups tend to be most at risk in extreme weather.

Individuals can adapt as well. Farmers can change how they plant and water crops. For example, they can choose methods that use less water. The climate crisis in the Northwest and Alaska is already serious. But many people there are taking action to help.

FOCUS ON
THE NORTHWEST AND ALASKA

Write your answers on a separate piece of paper.

1. Write a paragraph summarizing some of the harmful effects that climate change is having in the Northwest and Alaska.

2. Which solution described in Chapter 4 do you think is most helpful or important? Why?

3. How does El Niño affect the Northwest?

    A. It makes the Northwest hotter and drier.
    B. It makes the Northwest cooler and drier.
    C. It brings heavy rain and flooding.

4. Why might hot, dry weather help wildfires start and spread?

    A. Dried-out trees and plants can catch fire more easily.
    B. Dried-out trees and plants can take longer to burn.
    C. High temperatures help fires produce less smoke.

Answer key on page 32.

GLOSSARY

climate change
A human-caused global crisis involving long-term changes in Earth's temperature and weather patterns.

ecosystems
Communities of living things and how they interact with their surrounding environments.

Indigenous
Native to a region, or belonging to ancestors who lived in a region before colonists arrived.

infrastructure
The systems, such as roads, water supplies, and energy distribution, that a region needs to function.

ocean acidity
A human-caused change in the chemical properties of ocean water that causes coral skeletons and animal shells to weaken.

precipitation
Water that falls from clouds to the ground. It can be in the form of rain, hail, or snow.

toxins
Poisonous substances.

TO LEARN MORE

BOOKS

Harrison, Audrey. *Alaska*. Minneapolis: Abdo Publishing, 2023.

Kehoe, Rachel. *Improving Farming and Food Science to Fight Climate Change*. Lake Elmo, MN: Focus Readers, 2023.

London, Martha. *The Effects of Climate Change*. Minneapolis: Abdo Publishing, 2021.

NOTE TO EDUCATORS

Visit **www.focusreaders.com** to find lesson plans, activities, links, and other resources related to this title.

INDEX

Alaska, 11–12, 15–16, 18, 23, 25, 29

Boise, Idaho, 11, 27

Cascade Range, 9–11
Colville National Forest, 11, 13

Idaho, 11, 16, 25, 27

Lummi people, 13

Muckleshoot Indian Tribe, 20

Newtok, Alaska, 11, 23–24

Oregon, 5, 11, 16

Portland, Oregon, 5, 11, 28

Seattle, Washington, 5, 11, 28

Segrest, Valerie, 20

Sitka Tribe, 25

Washington, 5, 11, 13, 16, 20

Yup'ik people, 23

Answer Key: 1. Answers will vary; 2. Answers will vary; 3. A; 4. A